Women of Vice and Virtue

By Fay Mobley

© **Truth Publications, Inc. 2018. Second Printing.** All rights reserved. No part of this book may be reproduced in any form without written permission from the publisher. Printed in the United States of America

ISBN 13: 158427-217-1

ISBN 10: 978-158427-217-5

First Printing: 2007

Truth Publications, Inc.
CEI Bookstore
220 S. Marion St., Athens, AL 35611
855-492-6657
sales@truthpublications.com
www.truthbooks.com

Table of Contents

Introduction. 5
Lesson 1: Sarah—Princess, Mother of Nations 8
Lesson 2: Rebekah 12
Lesson 3: Leah and Rachel. 16
Lesson 4: Jochebed, Miriam, and Zipporah 20
Lesson 5: Bathsheba. 25
Lesson 6: Jezebel 28
Lesosn 7: Esther 31
Lesson 8: Mary—The Mother of Jesus. 35
Lesson 9: Mary and Martha 41
Lesson 10: The Samaritan Woman and Sapphira 47
Lesson 11: Lydia, Phoebe, and Dorcas. 52
Lesson 12: Lois, Eunice, and Priscilla 58
Lesson 13: Wives of Rulers 63

Women of Vice and Virtue

From the pages of Holy Writ comes the unfolding of the history and character of Bible women. As it is today, some were virtuous—worthy of praise and honor; others were women of vice. Their names conjure up in my mind's eye indelible images.

For example when I hear the name "Delilah," I see a deceived Samson, robbed on his strength and sight and, with one final vestige of strength, pull down a mightly structure. He dies as it falls.

"Jezebel" brings to my mind a picture of insatiable greed which robbed Naboth of his life. She was a constant and unrelenting enemy of Elijah and the people of God. Baal was her god and *evil* was her epitaph.

"Dorcas" creates an image of a room full of women whose mourning changes to rejoicing as Peter presents her to them alive and well, having raised her from the dead

I hear Eve's comfortless weeping as she learns that one son has been slain and the other one is his murderer.

I watch Jochebed as she weaves a basket of rushes, places her baby in the improvised ark, and sets him afloat in the Nile River, saving him from death at the hands of King Pharaoh

I listen as Priscilla assists her husband in teaching the eloquent Apollos "the way of the Lord more perfectly." I see Lois and Eunice as they teach the Holy Scriptures to young Timothy. "Sapphire" reminds me that God is not mocked and that all liars will have their part in the lake of fire.

The beautiful Bathsheba moves into my mind's view as a victim of circumstances, powerless to resist the advances of King David.

I see Deborah gently judging her people and shoring up the courage of Barak as he prepares for battle.

I imagine the sheer agony on the face of Mary as she watches her innocent, thorn-crowned Son die on the cross, knowing that he is dying for the very ones who placed him there.

Many other images enter my mind as I think of other Bible women. We know that the Scriptures were written for our learning, and we can profit greatly from our study of Bible women if we study with diligence and apply our knowledge with love and patience.

The following is a chart of ancestry dealing with some of the characters in our studies.

Adam		
Seth		
Noah		
Shem		
Terah		
Abraham and Sarah	Nahor	Haran
Isaac	Bethuel	Lot, Milcah, and Iscah Milcah married her uncle, Nahor. She is the mother of Bethuel (Gen. 11:29)
Jacob and Esau	Laban and Rebekah	Moab
	Rachel and Leah	Ruth

Jacob and Leah	Jacob and Rachel
Reuben	
Simeon	* Dan
Levi (ancestor of Moses, Aaron, and all priests under the law of Moses)	* Naphtali
	Joseph
Judah	Benjamin (ancestor of the apostle Paul)
* Gad	
* Asher	
Issachar	
Zebulun	
Dinah	
	* Sons of Bilhah, Rachel's handmaid
* Sons of Zilpah, Leah's handmaid	

Women of Vice and Virtue 7

Note: The twelve sons of Jacob became heads of the twelve tribes of Israel. This fact is very prominent in Bible history and it was sometimes necessary to "number" their descendants and to trace their ancestry in order to reap the benefits of being an Israelite and thus a child of God under the Old Testament era. The Israelites were a rebellious people and, when they were held captive by various "aliens," they sometimes lost their identity. It was necessary to reestablish it after returning to their own lands.

The map below shows the ancient world in which Abraham and his immediate descendants lived. Abraham lived in Hebron when he sent his servant to Mesopotamia (Padan Aram) to seek a wife for Isaac. The distance was approximately 600 miles "as the crow flies." The route which the servant took is not indicated in the Scriptures.

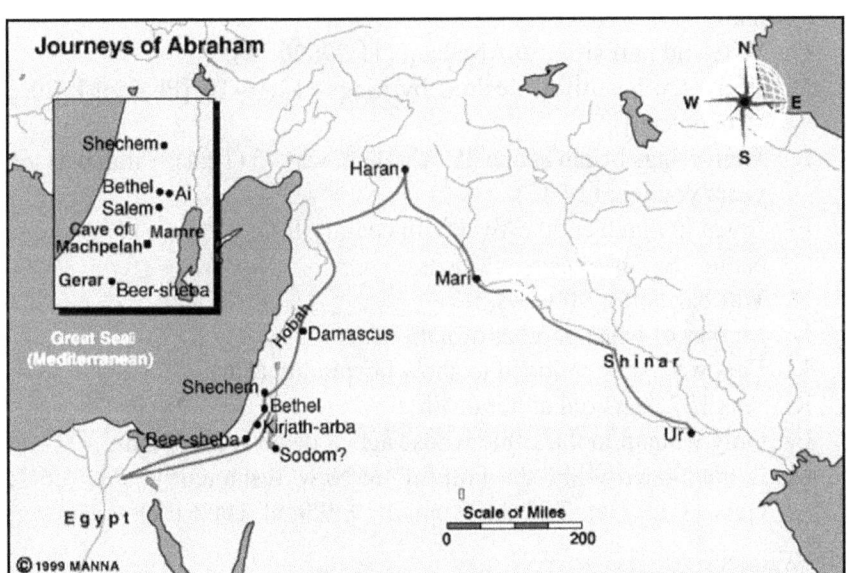

Lesson 1

Sarah—Princess, Mother of Nations
(Genesis 11-23)

I. Personal Data.
  A. Descendant of Seth (son of Adam) and Shem (son of Noah).
  B. The daughter of Terah (20:12). Did not have same mother as Abraham.
  C. Wife and half sister of Abraham (11:29; 20:12).
  D. Was very beautiful, desired by kings (12:14-16 [Pharaoh]; 20:2 [Abimelech]).
  E. Wanderings began at age 65. Abraham was 75 (12:4). Sarah was ten years younger (17:17).
  F. Lived in nineteenth or twentieth century B.C.
  G. Name "Sarah" means "Princess."
  H. Was barren for 90 years.
  I. Mother of Isaac, mother of nations.
  J. First woman mentioned to show hospitality (8:6).
  K. Was 127 years old at her death.
  L. Only woman in the Bible whose age at death is recorded.
  M. Is mentioned with "the faithful" in New Testament (1 Pet. 3:6-7; Heb. 11:11; Gal. 3:23-31; Rom. 4:19; 9:9; cf. Isa. 51:2).

II. Wanderings
  A. She traveled from Ur, between Persian Gulf and Bagdad, to Haran with Terah, Abraham, and Lot (11:31).
  B. At God's command, they left Haran to go to an unknown area (12:1).
    1. The "Great promise" was first given to Abraham at this time (12:2).
    2. Accompanied by Lot and his family, they eventually came to Canaan.
    3. Abraham built an altar built Shechem (Sichem), an important city in Palestine. At the time the Lord promised this land to his seed

(12:6-7).
C. Because of a famine, the family went to Egypt (12:10).
  1. For fear of his own life, Abraham passed Sarah off as his sister (12:11-15).
  2. This resulted in great plagues on the house of Pharaoh who had taken Sarah into his house (12:15-17).
  3. Sarah was then restored to Abraham and they were sent out of Egypt. They returned to Shechem (13:1-4).
D. Strife occurs between the herdsmen of Lot and Abraham (13:4-7).
  1. Abraham gave Lot his choice of the surrounding land (13:8, 9).
    a. Lot chose the rich plains of Jordan—Sodom (13:10-12).
    b. Abraham was left with the highlands—Canaan.
    c. The "Promise" was repeated to Abraham. He was told to walk through the land. It was to be given to his seed (13:17).
E. Abraham and Sarah move from the highlands to the plains of Mamre (13:18).
F. Lot was captured by kings who were "war mongers" and was rescued by Abraham and 318 of his servants (14:12-16).
G. On his return from the rescue, Abraham meets Melchizedek, king of Salem (Jerusalem), and priest of God. Abraham pays tithes to him and Melchizedek blesses Abraham.

III. Sarah's Intervention Into God's Promise.
A. She sent Abraham into her handmaid, Hagar (16:2-3). Hagar conceived.
B. When her conception are known, Hagar became obstinate, and was rebuked by Sarah (16:1-6).
C. Hagar fled and was told by God to return to Sarah (16:6-9).
D. God instructs Hagar concerning the name of her son and tells her he will be a "wild man" (16:11-12).
E. Ishmael was born when Abraham was 86 years old.

IV. The Promise.
A. When Abram was 99, his name was changed from Abram to Abraham (exalted father) (17:1-5).
B. The covenant of circumcision was introduced (17:10-14).
C. Sarah's name was changed from Sarai to Sarah and a son was promised to her (17:15-16).
D. Abraham, because of their ages, appealed to God that Ishmael be considered the son of promise (17:17-18).

- E. God denied Abraham's request but promised a blessing for Ishmael. (Ishmael means "God hears.")
- F. The covenant was established with Isaac who was to be born a year later (17:21).
- G. Abraham, Ishmael, and all the men of Abraham's house were circumcised when Abraham was 99 years old and Ishmael was 13 years old.
- H. Three men, messengers of God, were received hospitably by Sarah and Abraham (18:1-5).
  1. Sarah laughed at what she apparently thought was a ridiculous message. She was 89 years old and had always been barren. The angels announced that "Sarah, thy wife, shall have a son" (18:10-12). (Abraham had also "laughed" at the promiise, 17:17.)

V. Isaac (Isaac means "laughter").
- A. Isaac was born at the "set time" (21:1-2).
- B. He was circumcised on the eighth day according to the covenant (21:4).
- C. A feast was prepared by Abraham to celebrate his weaning (21:8).
  1. Ishmael and Hagar mocked Isaac (21:9).
  2. Sarah insisted that they be "cast out" (21:10).
  3. Abraham was reluctant to send them away but was convinced by God (21:11-13).
- D. Abraham was commanded to offer Isaac as a sacrifice (22:1-2).
  1. He prepared to obey God (22:3-10). He believed God would raise Isaac from the dead (Heb. 11:17-19).
  2. God intervened and furnished a ram for the offering.

VI. Death and Burial of Sarah.
- A. Sarah was 127 years old when she died (23:1-2).
- B. Abraham mourned her death. He bought the cave of Machpelah from Ephron, the Hittite, for a burial place (23:8-16).
- C. He buried Sarah in the cave (23:9) and was later buried there himself by Ishmael and Isaac (25:9).

Sarah—Princess, Mother of Nations

Questions

1. Sarah was the daughter of _____ (20:12).
2. How any children did she have? _____
3. How old was she at the birth of Isaac? _____
4. Who was her famous grandson? _____ His name was later changed to _____.
5. How was she related to her husband (20:12)? _____
6. Her name was changed from _____ to _____.
7. What desperate move did she make to "help" God? _____
   _____
8. Who was born of this union? _____
9. What "spoiled" the occasion of the weaning of Isaac for Sarah?
   _____
10. What did she demand as a result of this? _____
    _____
11. What did Abraham hope to gain by telling Pharaoh's servant that Sarah was his "sister"? _____
    _____
12. What does the name "Sarah" mean? _____
13. How did she react to the promise that she would be a mother?
    _____
14. How any times was she passed off as Abraham's sister? _____
15. Believing her to be his sister, what two kings took her into their courts? _____
16. What was the tragedy plaguing the life of Sarah? _____
17. What was the great miracle of her life? _____
    _____
18. Was she with Abraham when he paid tithes to Melchizedek?
    _____
19. Who was her famous nephew? _____
20. What relation was she to the illustrious Joseph? _____
    _____

Lesson 2

Rebekah
Genesis 24-28

Introduction

Rebekah was the great niece of Abraham. She was the grandaughter of Nahor and Milcah. Nahor was Abraham's brother and Milcah was his niece, a sister to Lot. Rebekah's father was Bethuel (Gen. 11:22-26; 24:15).

I. Rebekah was chosen to be the wife of Isaac in an unusual way (24:1-67).
   A. Abraham sent his servant to his country, Mesopotamia, to choose a wife for his son lest he take a wife of the daughters of the Canaanites (24:2-10).
   B. When the servant reached his destination, he prayed: "O Lord God of my master Abraham, I pray thee, send me good speed this day, and show kindness unto my master Abraham. Behold, I stand here by the well of water; and the daughters of the men of the city come out to draw water: and let it come to pass, that the damsel to whom I shall say, let down thy pitcher, I pray thee, that I may drink; and she shall say, Drink, and I will give thy camels drink also. Let the same be she that thou hast appointed for thy servant Isaac; and thereby shall I know that thou hast showed kindness unto my master" (Gen. 24:12-14).
      1. Before his prayer was finished, Rebekah came to the well and did exactly as he had prayed the chosen one would do.
   C. Blessed by her family, she returned to Canaan with the servant and became the wife of Isaac.

II. Rebekah's family (25:21-34).
   A. For twenty years, Rebekah was barren, but God granted Isaac's prayer in that she conceived and bore twin sons.
      1. Her first born was Esau, Isaac's favorite son who became a hunter.
      2. Jacob, Rebekah's favorite, lived in tents in the plains.
   B. A very hungry Esau came to the tent of Jacob from the fields and

begged food from him.
1. Jacob agreed to feed his brother providing Esau would pay for the food with his birthright (the first born son was always the major heir).
2. Esau agreed, thinking that his birthright would do him no good if he starved to death and left Jacob to inherit anyway (25:32-34).
3. Esau later married two Hittite women which caused his parents great sorrow.

III. Rebekah and Jacob's plot to deceive Isaac (27:1-29).
   A. Although Esau had sold his birthright to his brother, it was Isaac alone who would ultimately name his successor. Isaac requested that Esau prepare venison for him at which time he would bless his first born son.
   B. Rebekah, realizing that Esau was about to receive the blessing and wanting desperately for Jacob to be the one who was blessed, sent Jacob for two kids nearby.
      1. She prepared the savory dish and presented it to Isaac as though it were the venison he had requested.
      2. Isaac was blind but he recognized his sons through his other senses of feeling, hearing, and smelling. Thus Rebekah covered the smooth skin of Jacob's arms with the goat's skin to further confuse her blind husband (Esau's skin was hairy). Then she put the vestments of the first born on Jacob and together they confronted Isaac. All this was done while Esau was combing the fields for deer.
   C. The result of the deception.
      1. Believing Jacob to be Esau, Isaac bestowed the blessing upon Jacob (27:27-29).
      2. Upon learning that Jacob and Rebekah had deceived Isaac and that the blessing had been bestowed upon his brother, Esau threated Jacob's life.
         a. Rebekah learned of Esau's plans and she mapped out her strategy to send Jacob away for "a few days . . . until thy brother's fury turn away (27:44-45).
            (1) To Isaac she broached the subject of a suitable wife for Jacob. Lest he marry a Canaanite as did his brother, Isaac sent him to Rebekah's brother's home in Padan-aram, the plains region of Mesopotamia.

Conclusion

If we were telling this story to children we could not end it with the usual "and they lived happily ever after." Rebekah was never to see her beloved Jacob again. It would be twenty years before he returned to Canaan. She was to spend the remainder of her life with Esau and Isaac who knew she had deceived them.

Her two Hittite daughters-in-law were a constant source of grief to her as well (27:46).

Jacob, the deceiver, was to become Jacob, the deceived. First, Laban deceived him into thinking he was marrying Rachel—for whom he had worked seven years. Instead, he became the husband of Leah and was forced to work seven more years for Rachel to become his wife. Later in his life, his sons led him to believe that his beloved son, Joseph, had been killed by wild beasts. At this, Jacob said he would go to his grave mourning his son (Gen. 37:35).

Questions

1. What relation was Rebekah to Abraham?_____

    To Lot? _____ To Laban? _____

2. How many children did she have? _____

3. List the different ways in which she deceived her blind husband.

    _____

    _____

4. In what country did Isaac and Rebekah live?_____

5. True ____ False ____ Easu welcomed Jacob home when he returned.

6. What relation was Rebekah to Leah and Rachel other than mother-in-law?_____

7. True ____ False ____ Rebekah was barren for some twenty years before Jacob and Esau were born.

8. True ____ False ____ Polygamy was quite common during this era of Bible history.

9. Through which of Rebekah's sons was the promise given to Abraham to

be fulfilled (i.e., which was the ancester of Christ) (see Matt. 1:1-2).

_____

_____

10. Jacob's name was later to be changed to _____ and the _____ were his descendants.

Lesson 3

Leah and Rachel
Genesis 29-35

Leah and her younger sister, Rachel, were daughters of Laban, brother to Rebekah. They were cousins of Jacob.

Jacob had been sent by his parents to the home of Laban to choose a wife. His mother, Rebekah, had been chosen for Isaac from this same place. Upon his arrival in Laban's territory, Jacob met Rachel when she came to the well to water her father's sheep. She introduced him to her father who welcomed his kinsman and invited him to stay in his home. After a month had elapsed, Jacob and Laban negotiated Jacob's service. He agreed to work for Laban seven years for which the beautiful Rachel would be given to him to wed.

Jacob's seven-year service seemed "but a few days, for the love he had for her" (29:20). When he had fulfilled his seven years, he requested that Laban keep his part of the agreement. Pretending to comply, Laban made a feast that was to last seven days to which he invited the men of the community. After dark, he took Leah—not Rachel—to Jacob's quarters. Thinking the "tender-eyed" Leah was Rachel, Jacob "went in unto her" and did not discover the deception until morning. (It is likely that the bride was heavily veiled and the bridal chamber was very dark.)

When Jacob discovered that it was Leah rather than his beloved Rachel whom Laban had given to him, he confronted Laban with the trickery. Laban excused himself by saying it was "not so done in our country, to give the younger before the first born," but he agreed to give him Rachel also if he would work another seven years for him. Thus both Rachel and Leah became wives of Jacob.

Leah bore four sons: Reuben, Simeon, Levi, and Judah, but Rachel was barren. She blamed Jacob for her barren condition (30:1), and was rebuked by Jacob for her accusation. Like her kinswoman, Sarah, she decided to give Jacob her handmaid, Bilhah, hoping to "have children by her" (30:3). Bilhah bore two sons whom Rachel named Dan and Naphtali.

Leah and Rachel

Taking her cue from Rachel and believing herself to have become barren also, Leah gave her handmaid, Zilpah, to Jacob. She, too, bore two sons, Gad and Asher. According to the traditions of the time, children born to handmaids belonged to their mistresses. Thus Zilpah's sons were Leah's and Bilhah's sons were Rachel's.

Leah resented Jacob's love for Rachel and Rachel envied Leah's ability to bear children, so they were often at odds with one another. A case in point is their argument over mandrakes brought in by Leah's son, Reuben. Mandrakes were plum-sized fruit, the roots of which were reputed to promote conception. Both women seemed to be suffering from barrenness at this time. Rachel requested that the mandrakes be given to her to which Leah replied: "Is it a small matter that thou hast taken my husband? And wouldest thou take away my son's mandrakes also?" Rachel answered: "Therefore he (Jacob) shall lie with thee tonight for thy son's mandrakes" (30:15). Leah then bore her fifth son, Issachar and later her sixth son, Zebulun. She also bore her daughter, Dinah. It was after all Leah's children were born that Rachel gave birth to her first born son, Joseph, destined to become Jacob's favorite and a very prominent character in Israel's history,

After Joseph's birth, Jacob decided to go home. His shepherding had helped to enlarge Laban's flocks and herds greatly, but apparently he had none of his own.

He bargained with Laban for the "speckled, spotted, and black (ASV) cattle, sheep and goats" (30:25-32). With God's help and Jacob's expertise in animal husbandry, his flocks and herds grew to great proportions, angering Laban and his sons to the extent that Jacob thought it wise for him and his family to "steal away unawares" (31:1-21).

After three days, Laban learned of their leaving and pursued them, finding them in seven days. For some reason unspecified in the Scriptures, Rachel had taken the idol gods worshiped by her father. Laban searched all the belongings of Jacob but failed to find the gods which were hidden under Rachel's saddle (31:34). We learn later that Jacob hid the idol gods under the oak at Shechem (35:4). Through Jacob's psychological appeal, Laban was appeased and returned to his home in peace, while Jacob's family proceeded on their homeward journey.

When they neared Jacob's homeland, he feared his brother Esau, who had threatened his life twenty years earlier. His fears were unwarranted because Esau welcomed him "with open arms."

At this time, Rachel was with child. Her time for delivery came near when they approached Ephrath (Bethlehem) where she died giving birth to Benjamin, Jacob's twelfth and last son. Many centuries later, Matthew wrote: "In Rama was there a voice heard, lamentation, and weeping, and great mourning, Rachel weeping for her children, and would not be comforted, because they are not" (Matt. 2:18). Rama was a town between Judah and Israel which had been depopulated by Babylonian captivity. It was later repeopled by descendants of Benjamin (Neh. 11:31-33).

During their sojourn, Leah also had heartaches. Her daughter, Dinah, was raped by Shechem, the son of Prince Hamor. She was taken to his home but was later taken away by her brothers who killed Shechem for his defilement of their sister.

Rachel was loved, desired, and honored. Her sons played a very prominent part in biblical history. Joseph was to become an official in Pharaoh's Egyptian kingdom. It was to him that the world appealed for food when a devastating famine occured many years later and he was the sustainer during the seven-year period when food was not available anywhere else. Leah's sons who had treated him so shamefully would be at his mercy. Benjamin, Rachel's youngest, was the ancestor of a great tribe of whom the great apostle Paul was a descendant. However, it was from Leah's son, Levi, that the priesthood was established during the Mosaic age, and from Leah's son, Judah, came the world's Redeemer.

Questions

1. True _____ False _____ Rachel was an ancestor of Jesus.
2. True _____ False _____ Leah died in childbirth near Bethlehem.
3. Jacob worked _____ years for Rachel.
4. Jacob's love for _____ surpassed his love for _____.
5. Jacob's sons became fathers of the _____ tribes of Israel.
6. Name the sons of Leah and her handmaid.

   _____   _____
   _____   _____

7. Name the sons of Rachel and her handmaid.

   _____   _____
   _____   _____

Leah and Rachel

8. Leah was said to be "_____ _____" (29:17)
9. Rachel was _____ and well _____ (29:17).
10. Whom did Jacob fear as he neared his homeland? _____ Why?
    _____

    _____

11. Name one well-known New Testament character who was a descendant of Rachel _____; a descendant of Leah _____.

Lesson 4

Jochebed, Miriam, and Zipporah
Exodus 2, 15; Numbers 12,20

Background Information

Joseph, the favorite son of Jacob, was sold by his jealous brothers to Ishmaelites who, in turn, sold him to Potiphar, the captain of King Pharaoh's guard in Egypt (Gen. 37:27-28; 36). Joseph served Potiphar faithfully but, because he rejected the advances of Potiphar's wife, she made a false report to her husband which caused him to place Joseph in prison (Gen. 39).

While in prison Joseph, with the help of God, interpreted dreams for two fellow prisoners who were servants of Pharaoh. Later Pharaoh himself had a dream which Joseph was called upon to interpret. The dream revealed seven years of plenty followed by seven years of famine. Having won Pharaoh's trust, Joseph was made governor and was responsible for providing adequate storage facilities in preparation for the prophesied seven-year famine. Egypt thus escaped the consequences of the famine and became the only source of food during that time (Gen. 42). This was the occasion that brought Joseph's family—the Israelites—from Canaan to Egypt. They settled in the land of Goshen in Egypt and were well treated by the Egyptian government." Eventually, however, another Pharaoh "who knew not Joseph"(Exod. 1:8) became king and he made slaves of the Israelites.

Jochebed

It was during the enslavement that Jochebed was born. She and her husband were descendants of Levi (Num. 26:59; Exod. 6:19-20). From this tribe came all of the priests who officiated under the law of Moses. Aaron, their son, was the first to so serve after the law of Moses was initiated.

Because the population of the Israelites was growing so rapidly, and for fear that they would revolt and join his enemies, Pharaoh issued an edict that all males born to the Hebrews should be killed (Exod. 1:9-22). Moses was born to Jochebed during this time. She managed to hide him for three months (Exod. 2:3). When it became impossible to hide him any longer, she took an ark of bulrushes, made it waterproof, put Moses in it, and placed it in "the flags by the river's (Nile) brink" (Exod. 2:3).

Miriam, Jochebed's daughter, is introduced to us at this point in the Scriptures. She watched as Moses was placed in the river and stood guard until he was discovered by Pharaoh's daughter who had come to the river to bathe. Miriam asked this daughter of the king, "Shall I go and call to thee a nurse of the Hebrew women, that she may nurse the child for thee?" (Exod. 2:7). She then called her mother who became nurse to her own beloved son.

The Scriptures do not reveal how long Jochebed lived after this event. Whether or not she lived to see her son Moses become the great law giver, or if she knew what the destinies of her children were, we cannot know. It is reasonable, however, to conclude that she instilled in them the knowledge of and appreciation for the one true God.

Jochebed is mentioned by name only two times in the Scriptures (Exod. 6:20 and Num. 26:59). Nonetheless, her place in Bible history is very significant. She was the mother, not only of one of the world's greatest prophets, but also of the first priest ever to officiate under the Old Testament system of religion, as well as the mother of Miriam, the prophetess (Exod. 15:20).

Jochebed has much in common with the mother of Jesus. The lives of both baby Moses and baby Jesus were threatened by kings (Exod. 1:9-22; Matt. 2:13,16). Both sons were great prophets—one as the servant of God; the other as his Son. Both were deliverers from bondage; one from bondage to Egypt, the other from bondage to sin. Both were descendants of Jacob; both were law givers, etc. Jochebed's son, Aaron, was high priest under the Old Testament law; Mary's son is high priest under the New Testament law.

Miriam

During the time that Moses spent in the palace of Pharaoh and his subsequent forty years in Median, nothing is said of Miriam. She next comes upon the scene as a "prophetess" (Exod. 15:20), a woman inspired to teach the word of God. At this time the children of Israel had just crossed the Red Sea into the Wilderness of Shur, and Miriam composed a song of deliverance. This is reputed to be one of the earliest songs in Hebrew literature.

Miriam's character later changed from Miriam, the thankful, to Miriam the envious. She not only was envious of Moses' position, she was also vexed about his having married an Ethiopian woman (Zipporah had apparently died and Moses had remarried; Zipporah was a Midianite).

And Miriam and Aaron spake against Moses because of the Ethiopian woman whom he had married: for he had married an Ethiopian woman. And they said, hath the Lord indeed spoken only by Moses? Hath he not spoken also by us? And the Lord heard it. (Now the man Moses was very meek, above all the men which were upon the face of the earth). And the Lord spake suddenly unto Moses and unto Aaron, and unto Miriam, Come out ye three unto the tabernacle of the congregation. And they three came out. And the Lord came down in the pillar of the cloud, and stood in the door of the tabernacle, and called Aaron and Miriam: and they both came forth. And he said, Hear now my words: If there be a prophet among you, I the Lord will make myself known unto him in a vision, and will speak unto him in a dream. My servant Moses is not so, who is faithful in all mine house. With him will I speak mouth to mouth, even apparently, and not in dark speeches, and the similitude of the Lord shall he behold: wherefore then were ye not afraid to speak against my servant Moses? And the anger of the Lord was kindled against them; and he departed. And the cloud departed from off the tabernacle: and, behold, Miriam became leprous, white as snow: and Aaron looked upon Miriam, and, behold, she was leprous (Num. 12:1-10).

Aaron pleaded Miriam's case with Moses and Moses, in turn, who had once been temporarily smitten with leprosy himself (Exod. 4:6), asked the Lord to heal her (Num. 12:13). The Lord granted Moses' request but required that she be put out of the camp seven days according to the regulation regarding leprous people.

The final scene in Miriam's life takes place in Kadesh where she died and was buried (Num. 20:1). Like her brothers, she did not reach the promised land but, so far as the record goes, she remained faithful to God after the cleansing of her leprosy.

Zipporah (Exod. 2:21; 4:25; 13:2)

Zipporah was one of the seven daughters of Jethro who met Moses shortly after he fled for his life for having slain an Egyptian task master (Exod. 2:11). He found Zipporah and her sisters at a well in Midian where they had come to draw water for their father's sheep. The courteous Moses gave water to their sheep which earned him the respect and hospitality of Jethro, a priest.

Zipporah's marriage to Moses is recorded in seven words in Exodus 2:21. She bore him two sons, Gershon and Eliezer (Exod. 10:3-4). There is no evidence that she had any regard for her husband's religious convictions or that she played any part in his work or in his trememdous hardships. However, when Moses started back to Egypt from Midian on the mission God had appointed, Zipporah and their sons accompanied him. When they

Jochebed, Miriam, and Zipporah

stopped at an inn, Moses was met by the Lord who "sought to kill him" (Exod. 4:24). We cannot say for sure why this happened, but we can surmise from the context that Zipporah had thus far refused to have her son circumcised—a requirement for God's people at this time. "Zipporah took a sharp stone, and cut off the foreskin of her son, and cast it at his feet, and said, surely a bloody husband thou art to me" (Exod. 4:25). She repeated her accusation in verse 26.

What part Zipporah played in Moses life after this incident, we do not know. She is mentioned for the last time when she, her sons, and her father joined Moses at Mt. Horeb (Exod. 13:5). The text of Numbers 12:1 where Moses' Ethiopian wife is mentioned leads us to believe that Zipporah was dead at that time.

Questions

1. Jochebed was the mother of _____, _____, and _____.
2. She was the wife of _____, of the tribe of _____.
3. T____ F____ Miriam became her brother's nurse after he was discovered by Pharaoh's daughter.
4. At a very young age, Moses was considered a _____ child (Exod. 2:2, 10),
5. Why did Jochebed place Moses in a basket in the Nile River? _____
   _____
6. Through what process did Jochebed become her son's nurse? _____
   _____
7. T____ F____ Moses did not know he was of the Israelite nation while he was growing up in Pharaoh's palace.
8. In the life of Jochebed, in what way(s) do you see the providence of God manifested? _____
   _____
9. T____ F____ Miriam was a prophetess.

10. Miriam composed a song to celebrate the Israelites' _____ after they had crossed the Red Sea.
11. Why was Miriam unhappy with Moses? _____
    _____
12. T____ F____ Miriam died of leprosy because of her presumptuous sin.
13. T____ F____ Moses used Miriam as an example to teach obedience (Deut. 24:9).
14. Zipporah was the daughter of _____, a Midianite.
15. T____ F____ Zipporah was a shepherdess.
16. Moses met Zipporah at a well. Name some other Bible men who met their wives at wells (see Gen. 24:10, 11, 15; 29:10). _____
    _____
    _____
17. T____ F____ Zipporah was reluctant to allow her son to be circumcised.
18. To whom was the law of circumcision originally given (Gen. 17:10-14)? _____
19. What was the penalty for failing to comply with the law of circumcision (Gen. 17:14)? _____
    _____

Lesson 5

Bathsheba
2 Samuel 11:3; 12:24;
I Kings 1:11, 15, 16, 28, 31; 2:13, 18, 19

We are introduced to Bathsheba in 2 Samuel 11:2. Her husband, Uriah, one of King David's most trusted soldiers, was fighting the Ammonite war. The setting for the opening scene of her story is her home and the time is evening. Bathsheba was bathing in her Jerusalem home. David's new palace comanded a view of her house. He had gone out on his rooftop where he saw her washing herself and was immediatley attracted to her. "David sent messengers, and took her; and she came in unto him, and he lay with her . . . and she returned unto her house" (2 Sam. 11:4). According to the laws, Bathsheba could not have resisted had she wanted to, for a woman in those ancient times was completely subject to a king's will. It is very possible that David would have had her put to death had she refused to come to him. We have no indication of Bathsheba's thoughts or feelings in the matter. "I am with child" (2 Sam. 11:5) was the message she sent to David and she left him to deal with the situation.

David acted quickly and treacherously toward Bathsheba's husband. First he called Uriah to Jerusalem and insisted that he go down to his wife, but Uriah slept in his barracks with his men. Still, eager to throw the burden of the pregnancy on Bathesheba's husband, David tried a second time to get Uriah to go to his wife. But the conscientious, deeply consecrated soldier told David that he could not do that while the other soldiers were encamped in the open field. There was a law which forbade intercourse to warriors who had been consecrated for battle (1 Sam. 21:4). David then made Uriah drunk, thinking that he would surely go to his wife in that condition, but Uriah refused. Realizing that Uriah had no intentions of going to his wife, David ordered that he be placed in the forefront of the hottest battle and Uriah died in that battle at David's order. Bathsheba, we are told, "mourned for her husand" (2 Sam. 11:2).

A son was born of the adulterous union of David and Bathsheba and died after Uriah was killed. David then takes Bathsheba for his wife. Four sons are born to them. She interceded for her own son's succession to David's throne.

David's son, Adonijah, later asked Bathsheba to appeal to Solomon for him that he might have one of David's concubines for himself. When she appeared before Solomon, he said to her, "Ask on, my mother: for I will not say thee nay" (1 Kings 2:20). But he did say "nay," and even ordered Adonijah's death. Solomon is famous for his wisdom, and he no doubt knew that it was an ancient Semitic custom that the man who inherited the women of the dead king was his successor. Nonetheless, it appears that in honoring Adonijan's request to intercede for him, Bathesheba demonstrated kindness and Solomon's "I will not say thee nay" seems to say that he honored his mother greatly.

Though the adulterous union between Bathesheba and King David bore very dire consequences, she lives on today as the honored and serene mother of Israel's wisest king, and as one who gained her husband's favor, as well as one who was "very beautiful to look upon." Whether or not she ever knew that David had ordered her husband's death, we do not know. The Bible is silent in this regard.

Questions

1. Bathsheba was the daughter of _____.
2. She was the wife of _____, the Hittite.
3. She entered into an adulterous relationship with _____.
4. T____ F____ The child born of this adulterous union was named Solomon.
5. T____ F____ Solomon was the only living son of Bathsheba.
6. It was contrary to the law of the land for Bathsheba to reject David's advances because he was the _____.
7. Who rebuked David for his sins and how did he do it? (See 2 Sam 12: use your own words.) _____
   _____
   _____

Bathesheba 27

8. David was told that, although he would not die as a result of his sins, the _____ would never depart from his house,

9. T____ F____ Uriah was a trusted soldier in David's army.

10. David ordered that Uriah be placed in the _____ of the battle. Why? _____

11. T____ F____ The Scriptures say of Bathsheba that she was very much in love with David.

12. Bathsheba had _____ sons whose names were _____, _____, _____, and _____.

13. With the help of Nathan, she secured the throne for _____ over the futile attempts of Adonijah, another of David's sons.

14. T____ F____ Bathsheba is one of the ancestors of Jesus (see Matt. 1).

15. The Scriptures teach that man is tempted by being "drawn away of his own _____." Then when _____ conceived, it brings forth _____ and _____ and when it is finished, brings forth _____ (Jas. 1:14-15). Does this description of sin fit David? ____

16. True____ False____ The Scriuptures indicate that Bathsheba deliberately enticed David by "parading around naked."

17. Bathsheba was David's only wife. Yes____ No____.

18. True____ False____ David repented of his sins and confessed that they were "ever before me."

(Note: Many philosophers believe that Solomon wrote Proverbs 31:10-31 in honor of his mother. We have no way of knowing this, but we do know that she had won the respect of David when she made the entreaty for Solomon to succeed him, for David said ". . . assuredly Solomon thy son shall reign after me" (1 Kings 1:29-30). The fact that Nathan, the prophet of God, worked with her in securing the throne for Solomon also speaks well of her.)

Lesson 6

Jezebel

Because of Solomon's disobedience in turning to other gods, God said he would take all but one tribe from Solomon's son and give them to his servant. Thus, after Solomon's death, the kingdom was divided, with Rehoboam (Solomon's son) ruling southern Judah and Jeroboam (the son of one of Solomon's servants) being king over northern Israel.

During Jeroboam's twenty-two year reign, idolatry was firmly established in the kingdom of Israel. Fearing that the Israelites would return to Rehoboam, if they were allowed to return to Jerusalem to worship (as they were commanded to do by God), Jeroboam set up altars in Dan and Bethel where he instructed his subjects to offer sacrifices to idol gods. Being prone to listen to men instead of God, Israel obeyed the voice of their king.

Some forty years after Jeroboam began his reign, Ahab became Israel's ruler. His wife was the evil Jezebel. "And it came to pass, as if it had been a light thing for him to walk in the sins of Jeroboam the son of Nebat, that he took to wife Jezebel the daughter of Ethbaal, king of the Zidonians, and went and served Baal, and worshipped him" (1 Kings 16:34b).

Jezebel plotted and worked against everything that was right. She had no compunction whatsoever against murder, idolatry, greed, seduction, or any other evil that the mind can conjure up. She entertained 450 prophets of Baal, plus 400 prophets of "the grove" or Asherah at one time (1 Kings 18:19). It was to these prophets that God's prophet Elijah proposed a test. He asked that they gather on Mt. Carmel and build two altars: one for a sacrifice to Baal and the other for a sacrifice to Jehovah. He spoke to the people gathered there and asked, "Now long halt ye between two opinions? If the Lord be God, follow him: but if Baal, then follow him." He then proceeded to have Baal's prophets call upon their god, which they did from morning until noon. At noon, Elijah mocked them, saying Baal might be on a journey or asleep and they should call louder. They continued their quest for Baal until evening with no response. Then Elijah requested that the altar he had built for God be drenched three times with water, and at his first plea, God rained down fire that consumed the altar and lapped up the water that had been poured into the ditch around it. "And all the people

Jezebel

saw it, they fell on their faces; and they said, The Lord, he is the God" (1 Kings 18:39). Then Elijah instructed them to slay the prophets of Baal; none escaped. Jezebel's reation to the news that all her prophets had been slain is found in 1 Kings 19:2, "Then Jezebel sent a messenger unto Elijah, saying, So let the gods do to me, and more also, if I make not thy life as the life of one of them by tomorrow about this time." Of course she failed to carry out her threat and, since her gods were figments of her imagination, they could do nothing either for her or to her.

Naboth, a Jezreelite, had inherited a vineyard which bordered Ahab's palace grounds. Ahab wanted it for an herb garden and he offered to buy it. Naboth would not sell (see Num. 36:7). Ahab was pouting about this until Jezebel offered a solution to his problem. "I will give thee the vineyard of Naboth," she said (1 Kings 21:7). She wrote letters, using Ahab's seal, and dispatched them through servants stating that Naboth be accused of blasphemy. Two false witnesses were to testify against him, thus sealing his doom. Blasphemy, she knew, was punishable by stoning to death. This treachery was expedited to the letter and Jezebel calmly reported to her husband that Naboth was dead and the vineyard he coveted was his.

It was while Ahab was in Naboth's vineyard that Elijah told him how both he and Jezebel would die. ". . . in the place where dogs licked the blood of Naboth shall dogs lick thy blood. . . . the dogs shall eat Jezebel by the wall of Jezreel" (1 Kings 21:19-23). God's word never fails. Ahab was killed in battle and the dogs licked his blood. Jezebel was thrown from her window while chiding the prophet of God. When servants went to get her body to bury it, nothing was left but her skull, her feet, and the palms of her hands (2 Kings 9:35). The dogs had eaten her flesh.

That the name "Jezebel" is synonymous with evil is seen in Revelation 2:20 where it is used to refer to a heretical and idolatrous influence.

Jezebel was the daughter of a king, the wife of a king, and the mother of kings, but there was no godly royalty in her character. She was truly a woman of vice—with no virtue?

Questions

1. _____, the prophet of God, was a constant "thorn" in Jezebel's side.

2. Jezebel was the wife of _____ (1 Kings 18:31).

3. T____ F____ Jezebel suggested a contest between God's prophets and her prophets.

4. She was the daughter of _____ (1 Kings 16:11).

5. T____ F____ Jezebel's influence lived on in her daughter Athaliah, and was carried over into Judah when Athaliah became the wife of Jehoram, Judah's king (2 Kings 8:16-19).

6. Jezebel's god was _____.

7. According to the law of Moses, blasphemy was punishable by _____. How do you know (see Lev. 24:16; John 10:31-33)?_____
   _____

8. Jezebel was the daughter of the king of _____, the wife of the king of _____, the mother of the kings of _____, and the mother of the queen of _____.

Thought Question: What can we learn from our study of Jezebel that will help us to be what God would have us be?_____
_____
_____
_____
_____

Lesson 7

Esther
Esther 2-10

After King Ahasuerus deposes Vashti, his servants suggest that young virgins be brought to the palace from all his 127 provinces and that he choose one of them to take Queen Vashti's place (2:2-4).

Esther was an orphan Jewess of the tribe of Benjamin whose family had been captured by King Nebuchadnezzar of Babylon when Jeconiah (or Jehoiachin) was king of Judah (2:7). Her cousin, Mordecai, had reared her as his own daughter (2:5-7). Mordecai was an official at the palace who, at one time, through Esther, revealed a plot to Ahasuerus regarding two of his servants who sought to "lay hands on the king" (6:2). The result was that they were hanged.

When Mordecai learned of the king's plan to select a queen, he sent Esther to the palace to join many other maidens for the king's inspection. She subsequently became the "winner of the beauty contest" and her coronation was celebrated with a great feast which introduced her as queen of one of the most powerful empires on earth (2:17). Her name was changed from the Hebrew Hadassah (meaning "myrtle") to Esther (meaning "star").

Esther's sound judgment, self-control, and concern for others soon gained her favor with the people and she became a trusted confidant of her servants. Thus it was not long before she learned that her husband's favorite official, Haman, was intent upon destroying her people and that a serious feud was in progress between him and Mordecai.

After receiving a message from Mordecai which read, "Who knoweth whether thou art come to the kingdom for such a time as this?" Esther mapped out her strategy with great courage which she hoped would save her people.
1. She quietly ordered all Jews in Shushan to fast and she and her servants joined them in the fast (4:16).
2. She made ready to go to the king to intercede for her people. "So I

will go in unto the king, which is not according to the law: and if I perish, I perish" (4:16). Remember that an invitation was needed before one could approach the king, and Esther had no such invitation (1:11).
3. Perhaps because Ahasuerus "loved her more than all the others, he received her graciously. She invited him and Haman to be her guests at a banquet (5:4) and they gladly accepted. At this feast, she invited them to another one the next day.
    a. Following the first banquet, Haman boasted of his acceptance by the queen and his promotion by the king. However, he is still angry with Mordecai and other Jews because they refuse to pay homage to him. At the suggestion of his wife, Zeresh, and others, he had gallows built upon which he planned to hang Mordecai.
    b. Meanwhile the king cannot sleep following the banquet and he commanded that the records be brought to him to read. He thus discovered that Mordecai was the one who had saved him from his servants who plotted to kill him. He asked what had been done to reward him, to which his servants answered, "nothing" (6:1-3). He then asked Haman's opinion regarding "the man whom the king delighteth to honor." Mistakeningly thinking the king meant to honor *him*, Hamen suggested that he be royally dressed, placed upon the king's own horse, and paraded through the street of the city. "Then the king said to Haman, make haste, and take the apparel and the horse, as thou hast said and do even so to Mordecai the Jew,that sitteth at the king's gate: let nothing fail of all that thou hast spoken" (6:10).
    c. After expediting the king's command, and still seething with rage and humiliation, Haman was ushered into the second of Esther's banquets.
4. At this banquet the king told Esther he would grant her any petition—"even to half of the kingdom" (7:2) that she requested.
    a. At this point Esther revealed her identity as a Jew, disclosed the plot against her people, exposed Haman as the adversary, and pleaded the case of her people with the king (7:3-6).
    b. Upon learning that Haman had built a gallows for Mordecai, Ahasuerus ordered that Haman himself be hanged on it; that his house be given to Esther, and that the ring he had given to Haman be given to Mordecai.This ring indicated authority second only to the king himself.
    c. Esther further requested that Haman's letters—which were sent out earlier requiring the death of the Jews—be rescinded. To this Xerxes agreed. He also granted them the liberty to fight against all who would assault them and to take the spoils of their assailants.

Esther

    d. Hence, "the Jews had joy and gladness . . . and many of the people of the land became Jews" (2:17). Mordecai, being advanced to the position of "next unto king Ahasuerus" sought the "good of his people," and spoke "peace to all his seed" (10:3).

    The feast of Purim was initiated by Esther and Mordecai wherein "portions" were given to one another and "gifts to the poor" (5:20-32). The Purim Festival is celebrated by Jews today on the 14th and 15th of March when the Roll of Esther is read in the synagogues.

    According to history, Ahasuerus was finally murdered by one of his own officers.

Questions

1. Esther was of the tribe of _____ (2:5) .
2. She replaced _____ as Queen (2:4, 17).
3. _____ was the Jews' enemy who was determined to hang Mordecai and destroy the Jews.
4. Why was he so angry with Mordecai and other Jews (3:2-5)? _____

5. Esther's Hebrew name was _____ (2:7).
6. What was Esther's relationship to Mordecai? _____
7. In what way did Haman die? _____

8. In your own words, tell how Esther interceded for her people. _____

9. True____ False____ Esther was the favorite one in the king's harem, therefore she was permitted an audience with the king at any time she chose.
10. Xerxes palace was called _____ (2:3).
11. What Jewish feast was introduced by Esther and Mordecai? _____

12. List as many of Esther's characteristics as you can which should also be possessed by Christian women today. _____

_____

_____

_____

Lesson 8

Mary, Mother of Jesus

Introduction

Mary was the daughter of Heli (Eli, Luke 3:23). Joseph was the son of Jacob (Matt. 1:16). Both are decendants of David—Mary through Nathan and Joseph through Solomon (Luke 3:31; Matt. 1:6). (See list of genealogies, 39)

Mary was the mother of Jesus, James, Joses, Juda, and Simon and "of daughters" (Mark 6:3). She is mentioned in the following Scriptures: Matthew 1-2; Luke 1-2; John 2:11-12; Matthew 12:46; Mark 3:21, 31ff.; John 19:25; Acts 1:14.

I. Birth of Jesus Announced (Luke 1:28-35).
   A. Mary lived in Nazareth, a city of Galilee (Luke 1:26).
   B. She was a virgin, espoused (engaged) to Joseph. The angel, Gabriel, appeared to her:
      1. Complimented her virtues—"Thou art highly favored, the Lord is with thee."
      2. Announced that she would conceive of the Holy Spirit.
      3. She was to give birth to a son whose name would be "Jesus."
      4. He would reign on the throne of David over the house of Jacob.
      5. There would be no end to his reign (see Dan. 2:44).
      6. Gabriel informed her that her cousin Elisabeth also was to give birth to a son.
      7. Mary humbly accepted this great honor—"Behold the handmaid of the Lord; be it unto me according to thy word" (Luke 1:38).

II. Mary's Visit to Elisabeth (Luke 1:39-56).
   A. Elisabeth was the wife of Zacharias, a priest.
   B. They lived in Judea (about 50 or 60 miles from Nazareth).
   C. The good news that Mary was to be the mother of the Lord prompted Elisabeth to say: "Blessed art thou among women, and blessed is the fruit of thy womb" (Luke 1:42).
   D. Mary gave all the honor to God (1:46-55).
   E. Mary remained with Elisabeth for three months. By this time Elisabeth's time of delivery was due, and she gave birth to John—later

known as John the Baptist or baptizer.
F. Mary returned to Nazareth and married Joseph (Luke 1:56).
   1. God had spoken to Joseph in a dream and explained Mary's condition to him. He instructed him to take her as his wife (Matt. 1:18-25).

III. Birth of Jesus.
   A. Caesar Augustus (27 B.C.- A.D. 14) decreed that all his subjects be taxed (Luke 2:1).
   B. All the inhabitants in Caesar's empire were required to go to the city of their forefathers to pay these taxes (Luke 2:4).
   C. Joseph, of the seed of David, was required to go to Bethlehem, the city of David (2:4).
   D. Mary accompanied Joseph to Bethlehem, fulfilling the prophecy that the Savior would be born in Bethlehem (Mic. 5:2; Matt. 2:6).

IV. King Herod's Reaction and Results.
   A. Wise men, who had been led by a star in the east came to Jerusalem and inquired in the city where they might find the "King of the Jews" (Matt. 2:1-2).
   B. Herod learned from the chief priests and scribes that he was in Bethlehem—"according to the scriptures" (Matt. 2:3-5).
   C. He instructed the wise men to find the Child and bring him information regarding his whereabouts—pretending that he also wanted to worship him.
   D. Herod's real purpose was to destroy the child whom he believed to be a threat to his political status—this "King of the Jews" (Matt. 2:13).

V. Flight Into Egypt and Nazareth (Matt. 2:13-23).
   A. Because of the jealousy of Herod and the threat to the life of Jesus, Joseph was instructed to take his family to Egypt where they remained until the death of Herod.
   B. When they learned that the wicked Archelaus reigned in Judea on his father's throne, they went to Nazareth instead of returning to Judea.

VI. Trip to Jerusalem (Luke 2:41-52).
   A. Went every year for the feast of the Passover (Luke 2:41; Exod. 23:15-17).
   B. Jesus accompanied them when he was twelve years of age.
   C. Jesus remained in Jerusalem when his parents left to return home.
   D. They traveled "a day's journey" before they missed him.

Mary, Mother of Jesus

    E. They found him after three days, in the temple talking with the doctors of the law.
    F. Mary rebuked Jesus for causing them such anxiety.
    G. Jesus, after asking *how* they had sought him, said, "Wist (know) ye not that I must be about my Father's business" or "Know ye not that I must be in my Father's house?" (Luke 2:49, ASV).
    H. They returned to Nazareth and Jesus was "subject unto them."
    I. Nothing more is revealed of the family until Jesus is about thirty years old and goes to John to be baptized.

VII. The Wedding Feast of Cana (John 2:1-11).
    A. Mary informed Jesus that the host was out of wine.
    B. She instructed the servants to do as he bid them.
    C. Jesus turned six waterpots of water into wine.
    D. This is the first recorded miracle performed by our Lord.

VIII. The Crucifixion (John 19:25-27)
    A. Jesus looked down from the cross and saw his mother standing beside the disciple whom he loved (probably John).
    B. He entrusted the care of her to this disciple—"Woman, behold thy son"; "Behold thy mother."
    C. Mary was, from that time on, cared for by this disciple.

IX. Conclusion.
    A. The last mention of Mary is found in Acts 1:14 where she is assembled with the apostles in Jerusalem.
    B. There is no biblical record of the time or manner of her death.

Questions

1. By whom was the birth of Jesus announced? _____
2. Where did Mary live at that time? _____
3. What does the word "espoused" mean? _____
4. How was Mary related to Elisabeth? _____
5. How was Jesus related to John? _____
6. Why did Mary and Joseph go to Bethlehem? _____

7. Angels announced Christ's birth to the _____
8. Why did the family to to Egypt? _____

9. What was Herod's decree concerning male children following the birth of Jesus? _____
10. Who had prophesied that Jesus would be born in Bethlehem? _____
11. Did Mary have other children? If so, what were their names? _____
12. Did Mary ever rebuke Jesus? If so, when? _____
13. Is there any evidence that Mary ascended into heaven? _____
14. Is there any evidence that she makes intercession for Christians? _____ Is there any evidence that she does not. _____ If so, what is the evidence and where is it found in the Scriptures? _____
15. How was she "blessed among women"? _____
16. Both Mary and Joseph are descendants of _____
17. To whom did Jesus entrust the care of his mother? _____
18. With whom is Mary found when she is last mentioned in the Scriptures? _____ Where? _____

Genealogies

Matthew (Joseph)	Luke (Mary)	
Abraham	Abraham	Simei
Isaac	Isaac	Mattathies
Jacob	Jacob	Maath
Judas (*Judah)	Juda (Judah)	Nagge
Phares	Phares	Esli
Esrom	Esrom	Naum
Aram	Aram	Amos
Aminadab	Aminadab	Mattathias
Naason	Naasson	Joseph
Salmon	Salmon	Janna
Booz (Boaz)	Booz	Melchi
Obed	Obed	Levi
Jesse	Jesse	Matthat
David	David	Heli
Solomon	Nathan	Joseph (son-in-
Roboam	Mattatha	law of Heli;
Abia	Menan	son of Jacob)
Asa	Melea	
Josaphat	Eliakim	
Joram	Jonan	
Ozias	Joseph	
Joatham	Juda	
Achaz	Simeon	
Ezekias	Levi	
Manasses	Matthat	
Amon	Jorim	
Josias	Eliezer	
Jehonias (Jehoiachin)	Jose	
Salathiel (grandson of Jehoiachin)	Er	
Zorobabel	Elmodam	
Abiud	Cosam	
Eliakim	Addi	
Azor	Melchi	
Sadoc	Neri (son-in-law of Jehoiachin)	
Achim	Salathiel (son of Jehoiachin's daughter)	
Eliud	Zorobabel	
Eleazar	Rhesa	
Matthan	Joanna	
Jacob	Juda	
Joseph (husband of Mary)	Joseph	

Matthew (Joseph)	Luke (Mary)
Note: "14 generations" from captivity to Christ (Matt. 1:17) necessitates that one count Salathiel as the grandson of Jechonias, rather than his son. This is born out in Luke's record where Neri, not Jechonias, is said to be the father of Salathiel. "The son of" often means the "descendant of" in the Scriptures. A case in point is Jesus—"the son of David," though 28 generations later.	**Note:** Jesus is the descendant of both Solomon and Nathan. Jehoiachin's daughter, a descendant of Solomon, married Neri, a descendant of Nathan. To this union was born Salathiel, of whom Jesus is descended. While this union is not mentioned specifically in the Scriptures, it is necessarily inferred when one looks at both genealogical records. This explanation is given in Bible dictionaries and in secular history.

Lesson 9

Mary and Martha

John 11:1-46; 12:1-4; Luke 10:38-42; Matthew 26:6-13; Mark 14:3-9

I. Backgrounds information.
   A. Mary and Martha were sisters who lived with their brother, Lazarus, in the small Judean village of Bethany which was located about fifteen furlongs (1.8 miles) from Jerusalem (John 11:18). It was on the Jericho Road at the foot of the Mount of Olives. These three were friends of Jesus who provided a "home away from home" for him. Obviously they were not poor.
   B. The marital status of these sisters is not known. Since no husbands are mentioned, it is most likely that (1) they had never been married, or (2) they were widows.
   C. The lives of Mary and Martha are so closely interwoven that it is impossible to study about one without involving the other. Let us look at the characteristics of both women and learn from their examples:
      1. Mary
         a. Believed Christ was Lord (John 11:32).
         b. Sought "first things first," things pertaining to the soul (Luke 10:42).
         c. Was humble in her worship (John 12:3).
      2. Martha
         a. Believed Christ was God's son and confessed this fact (John 11:27).
         b. Believed he could intercede with God (John 11:21-22).
         c. Was a conscientious worker (Luke 10:40).

II. Spiritual and Material Perspectives (Luke 10:38-42).
   A. Jesus was a guest in the house of Martha and Mary.
      1. Martha, the conscientious hostess, was "cumbered about with much serving."

       2. Mary, on the other hand, "sat at Jesus' feet, and heard his word."
    B. Jesus' evaluation of the situation.
       1. He did not rebuke Martha for being a conscientious hostess. He did call her attention to the fact that she was "careful and troubled about many things" while *one* thing was needful.
          a. While he was there with them, she needed to be concerned with the one thing—the only thing that "shall not be taken from her" (Luke 10:41-42)—to take advantage of the opportunity to sit at Jesus' feet and learn. There would be time later for material responsibilities to be done.
       2. Mary put things in the proper perspective. We can be sure that she was not a lazy or slothful homemaker. Rather, she recognized that spiritual food was far more important than food for the physical body and she availed herself of the opportunity to feed her soul. Jesus commended her actions.
    C. Application for us.
       1. "Seek ye first the kingdom of God and his righteousness" (Matt. 6:33).
       2. Examples of how we might stand rebuked as was Martha.
          a. Miss worship services to cook for guests.
          b. Be too "cumbered about" to take time to help someone in need.
          c. Be so concerned with an immaculate house that we fail to extend hospitality, etc.
       3. We are not to be slothful in homemaking (Tit. 2:3-5), but we must not make this our primary concern. Attending to our souls is to be our major goal; all materialistic responsibilities follow as we have time and opportunity.
       4. We cannot serve Jesus physically as did Martha, but we can "sit at his feet" as did Mary and serve him as he directs in his word.

III. Mary and Martha's appeal to Jesus for their brother, Lazarus (John 11:1-46).
    A. They sent a message to Jesus, "He whom thou lovest is sick" (11:3).
    B. Jesus purposely waited two days before going to their aid.
       1. He was staying in "a place beyond Jordan" (John 10:40).
       2. His disciples warned him that Jews in Judea sought his life, but he was not deterred.

Mary and Martha 43

3. He told his disciples that Lazarus "sleepeth; but I go that I may awake him." When they misunderstood, thinking that Lazarus was only asleep, Jesus told them plainly, "Lazarus is dead" (John 11:14).
C. The raising of Lazarus from the dead.
 1. Martha went out to meet Jesus and told him that Lazarus would not have died had he been there (11:21).
 2. When Jesus told her that he would rise again, she mistakenly thought he meant at the general resurrection. It was in answer to her that Jesus spoke the oft-quoted statement: "I am the resurrection and the life: he that believeth in me, though he were dead, yet shall he live" (11:25).
 3. "Jesus wept," the shortest verse in the Bible (11:35), demostrates the great compassion he has for our sorrows.
 4. Even though Lazarus had been dead four days, at Jesus' words, "Lazarus, come forth," he came forth from the grave.
   a. A preacher once said: "If Jesus had not said, '*Lazarus*, come forth,' he'd have emptied every cemetery in the world."
 5. Jesus' power is unlimited. Someday he will say, "Come forth" and he will empty every cemetery in the world (see Rev. 20:12-13; 1 Cor. 15:22).
D. Application for us.
 1. Jesus cares, he is touched with our grief. Therefore we can go to him for comfort (1 Pet. 5:7).
 2. Whether we have been dead for four days or centuries, at his words, "Come forth," we will be resurrected.
 3. Spiritually speaking, though "dead in sin," we can be "raised to life" (Col. 2:13) by him. He is continually saying, "come forth."

IV. Mary's anointing of Jesus (Matt. 26:6-13; Mark 14:3-9; John 12:3).
A. What was done?
 1. An alabaster box of ointment was broken by Mary (John 12:3) who poured the ointment on the head and feet of Jesus to prepare him for burial.
   a. Alabaster is a white stone used to ornament buildings, for vases, and in making bottles wherein precious liquids were kept. The box was broken, indicating that Mary intended to use all of it on Jesus.
   b. The ointment—spikenard—was a very costly ointment.

B. Where and when was it done?
1. In Bethany in the house of Simon the Leper while they "sat at meat."
   a. Lepers were required by the law of Moses to dwell apart from society (Lev. 13:46). Guests were being entertained in Simon's home, so he obviously is not living in seclusion at this time.
   b. There was no known cure for leprosy. Therefore, it is strongly suggested that Jesus had miraculously healed Simon and he is called "the leper" simply to distinguish him from others named Simon.
   c. Mary's deed was done prior to ("aforehand") Jesus' death, while she had the opportunity (another example of her priorities).
C. What were the results?
1. Some disciples, particularly Judas Iscariot, complained that this act was a "waste." It could have been sold and the proceeds given to the poor, he said.
   a. His motive was not concern for the poor. He was a "thief" (John 12:6).
2. Jesus' attitude was:
   a. She did a good work and her story would be told "wherever the gospel is preached." It is a matter of permanent record and wherever there is a Bible, there is Mary's good deed.
   b. He put the emphasis—once again—on the proper perspective.
      (1) There would always be the opportunities to help the poor.
      (2) The opportunity to do this good work to him would not always be available.
D. Some applications:
1. Present opportunities to do good should be taken advantage of (Gal. 6:10).
2. The value of a good deed is not measured in dollars and cents.
3. Jesus knows all our deeds and the good does not go unnoticed by him.
4. The time to do good to another is while he is alive. We can pay our respects to the dead, but it does them no service.
5. We must put things in the proper perspective; spiritual things first, then material things.

Mary and Martha 45

Questions

1. What was the "good part" that Jesus said Mary chose? _____
   _____

2. T____ F____ Both Mary and Martha believed Jesus was the Son of God (see John 11:27-32).

3. T____ F____ Lazarus, the brother of Mary and Martha, is the Lazarus of Luke 16:20.

4. Was Martha rebuked for being a conscientious hostess? _____ If not, what was her problem? _____
   _____

5. Thought Question: Mary could have helped Martha with the serving, then both could have "sat at Jesus' feet." What is wrong with this suggestion? _____
   _____

6. By what one statement in our lesson can we know that Jesus shares our sorrows? _____

7. T____ F____ Jesus teaches that homemaking is of little consequence. Explain your answer.

8. T____ F____ The monetary value of a deed or gift determines its worth.

9. Who led in the criticism of Mary when she anointed Jesus with spikenard? _____

10. T____ F____ Martha was skeptical of Jesus' power to raise her brother from the grave (see John 11:21-22).

11. What was the reaction of the chief priests and Pharisees to Lazarus' resurrection (see John 11:47-53). _____
    _____

12. Jesus purposely postponed going to Bethany when he received news that Lazarus was sick. Why? _____
    _____

13. Mary, Martha and Lazarus were sisters and brother in the flesh and were concerned about one another. How may we apply this to our

spiritual relationship? _____
_____

14. To what source did Mary and Martha go on behalf of their brother? _____ To what source should be go on behalf of our brother (or sister)? _____

15. Give some examples of how one makes the same mistake Martha made. _____
_____
_____

16. Give some examples of how we may choose "that good part" as did Mary. _____
_____
_____

Lesson 10

The Samaritan Woman and Sapphira

The Samaritan Women (John 4:1-29)

I. Jesus' meeting with the Samaritan Woman.
   A. He was on his way from Judea to Galilee (4:3).
   B. He had to pass through Samaria.
      1. Samaria was the ancient capital of the northern kingdom of Israel.
      2. Ahab and Jezebel had built a temple for Baal in Samaria; idolatry flourished.
      3. It was captured in 722 B.C. by the Assyrians.
      4. Jews of Samaria intermarried with Assyrians, thus creating a the Samaritan race.
      5. Samaritans in Christ's time were, for the most part, were half Jew and half Gentile.
      6. They sacrificed on Mt. Gerizim mixing heathen worship with their sacrifices (see John 4:22), while the Jews sacrificed in the temple in Jerusalem (4:20),
      7. The Samaritans were considered unclean by the Jews.
   C. Jesus came to the well which Jacob had dug near the city of Sychar (4:5-6). Weary from his travels, he sat down to rest.
   D. The Samaritan woman came to the well to draw water and he asked her for a drink.

II. The Two Waters.
   A. Water furnished by Jacob's well supplied only physical needs and served as a temporary relief from thirst (4:13—"will thirst again").
   B. Water which Jesus supplies sustains the spiritual body and is eternal in nature (4:14—"will never thirst").
   C. See also John 6:35; 7:38; and Matthew 5:6.

III. Jesus, the Prophet.
   A. In answer to Jesus' request that she call her husband, she said, "I have no husband." He told her she had had five husbands but the one she was living with was not her husband (4:16).
   B. It was this statement that convinced her that Jesus was a prophet.
   C. Her observation regarding worship (4:20).
      1. Samaritans worshiped "in this mountain" (Gerizim).
      2. "Ye say that in Jerusalem is the place where men ought to worship."
   D. Jesus' comments about true worship.
      1. The *place* where God is to be worshiped is no longer restricted to Jerusalem or the mountain of Gerizim.
      2. "In spirit and in truth" are the *essential* features of the true worship.

IV. Jesus, the Messiah, the Christ (4:25-29).
   A. "When he (the Messiash, the Christ) is come, he will tell us all things."
   B. "I that speak unto thee am he."
   C. "Come, see a man, which told me all things that ever I did: is not this the Christ?"

Conclusion

The Samaritan woman was an adulteress and an "outcast," but Jesus came to "seek and to save that which was lost" (Luke 19:10; 1 Tim. 1:15). His "living water" is still available to all who thirst for righteousness.

Sapphira (Acts 4:31-5:11)

I. The Occasion.
   A. At the time the church was established, the Law of Moses was in effect.
      1. Under that law, Jews were required to assemble in Jerusalem for the observance of three annual feasts. The Feast of Pentecost, or the feast of first fruits was one such occasion.
      2. Hence Jews "from every nation under heaven" (Acts 2:5) were assembled for the purpose of celebrating this feast.
      3. This was a most opportune time for the apostles to preach the gospel in its fulness for the first time.

The Samaritan Woman and Sapphira

II. The Need.
   A. It is quite possible that some of the Jews, after having witnessed the great outpouring of the Holy Spirit, and becoming obedient to the gospel, decided to remain in Jerusalem rather than return to their native homes.
      1. The church was a new institution; there was no other congregation in any other commuity where the new Christians could worship.
   B. Regardless of the circumstances which created a need, the fact that there was one is evident from Acts 4:33-37.

III. Christians Relieved the Need.
   A. There is no evidence that they were commanded to sell their lands. In fact, we know that this was a free choice from Peter's statement in chapter 5:4.
      1. Those who did sell their possessions were not required to give the entire proceeds to the church.
      2. They were (as are we) required to give as they had been prospered (1 Cor. 16:1-2).
   B. It was therefore by choice that "as many as were possessors of lands or houses sold them, and brought the price of the things that were sold and laid it at the apostles' feet: and distribution was made unto every man according as he had need" (4:34-35).

IV. Ananias and Sapphira's Conspiracy.
   A. They "conceived in their hearts" to pretend to give the entire proceeds from the sale of their possessions to the church.
   B. Keeping back "part of the price" was not their sin. It was theirs to do with as they chose both before and after it was sold (v. 4).
   C. Ananias' sin was lying to God, while Sapphira lied both to men and to God.
      1. Peter "read Ananias' mind" and knew of his planned deception. There is no record of his having *said* anything.
      2. Sapphira lied when she answered Peter's question (see v. 3). She had already lied to God (v. 2).
   D. Their punishment was physical death.
   E. Results: "Great fear came upon all the church, and upon as many as heard these things" (5:11).

V. Application.
   A. Discipline of unruly members of the church is necessary; it is commanded (see 2 Thess. 3:6; 1 Cor. 5:1-5).
   B. Lying will result in death (Rev. 21:8).
      1. Although no man can "read our minds" as Peter did, God can, and we can lie to him exactly like Ananias and Sapphire did. (Many do.)
   C. Their lying was done to impress people. As she did, so may we become so eager to impress people that we become hypocritical. In so doing we do not impress God. Jesus said, "Let your light so shine before men that others may see your good works. . . ." We sometimes prefer to shine our lights rather than let them shine.

NOTE: God's abhorrence of lying is shown in the fact that it was the first recorded sin in the Old Testament when the physical kingdom was new and the first recorded sin in the New Testament when the spiritual kingdom was new. Let us be impressed with the fact that we can lie to him without saying a word. Be not deceived; *God is not mocked* (Gal. 6:7).

Questions

1. Define "lie." _____
   _____

2. T____ F____ To help the needy, the Jersualem Christians were required to sell their possessions.

3. T____ F____ All Christians are, and always have been, required to give as prospered.

4. Name some ways in which we can be guilty of the same sins as Sapphira._____
   _____

5. Who caused this couple to "conceive this thing in their hearts"? ____
   _____

6. What does "being privy to it" (v. 2) mean? _____
   _____

7. True____ False____ Lying to men is not as serious as lying to God. Give reason for your answer. _____
   _____

The Samaritan Woman and Sapphira   51

8. What penalty did this couple pay for their sin? _____

9. What penalty will we pay for the same sin? Give Scripture(s) for your answer. _____
10. T____ F ____ Hypocrisy is a form of lying.
11. T____ F ____ The Jews ordinarily had no dealings with the Samaritans.
12. Jesus offered the Samaritan woman _____ water.
13. She had had _____ husbands but was, at that time, living with a man who was not her husband.
14. Samaritans worshiped in Mt. _____ while the Jews worshiped in _____ .
15. Jesus said true worshipers must now worship in _____ and in _____ .
16. True____ False____ Jesus did not tell the Samaritan woman that he was the Messiah.
17. What verses in this chapter show the human attributes of Jesus? ___ _____
18. What convinced the Samaritan woman that Jesus was the Christ? __ _____
19. Explain what Jesus meant by "living water." _____ _____
20. Jesus promised living water to all who _____ and _____ after righteousness (Matt. 5:6).

Lesson 11

Lydia, Phoebe, and Dorcas
Servants of God

Lydia (Acts 16)
I. Lydia was originally from Thyatira, a city in Lydia, a large country of Western Asia Minor, ninety miles northeast of Ephesus.
   A. One of John's famous letters in the Revelation was addressed to the church in Thyatira (Rev. 2:18-19).

II. At the time of her conversion, Lydia lived in Philippi, a city of Macedonia on the continent of Europe.
   A. She and her companions were encountered by Paul, Silas, Luke, and Timothy while Paul was on his second missionary journey.
   B. They were the first to be taught the gospel after the vision appeared to Paul while he was in Troas: "Come over into Macedonia and help us" (Acts 16:9).

III. Lydia was a seller of purple—a lucrative business.
   A. We do not know whether she sold the dye or the textiles.
      1. The purple dye was made from "madder root" which grew abundantly in Thyatira. It was also extracted from certain types of shell fish.
      2. Purple fabric were worn primarily by royalty and the very rich (see Luke 16:19). It was placed on Jesus in mockery (as the *king* of the Jews) prior to his crucifixion (Mark 15:17).

IV. Lydia and her friends were gathered by riverside (the River Gangites—modern Angista) where "prayer was wont to to be made."
   A. This occurred on the Sabbath as required by the law of Moses.
   B. This is where Paul and his company joined them, perhaps aware that worship was taking place there.
   C. They proceeded to teach them the gospel which she and her household received.

D. After her baptism, Lydia insisted that they come into her home "if ye have judged me to be faithful to the Lord."
  1. The Lord opened her heart; she opened her home to his messengers.

V. While abiding in the house of Lydia, Paul cast an evil spirit out of a "soothsayer."
  A. Along with Silas, he was beaten and cast into prison.
  B. At midnight they prayed and sang and an earthquake opened the prison doors.
  C. They taught and baptized the jailor and his household.
  D. Then they returned to the house of Lydia.

VI. So far as the record goes, Lydia was the first convert on the continent of Europe and the first member of the church in Philippi.

Phoebe (Rom. 16:1-2)

I. "Phoebe, our sister."
  A. "Our sister" denotes her relationship to Paul and the Christians at Rome.
  B. All Christians are members of the universal church, children of God and thus brothers and sisters in Christ. Although the Roman Christians had not heretofore known Phoebe, she was nonetheless their sister just as she was Paul's.

II. "A servant of the church at Cenchrea."
  A. It is quite likely that Phoebe delivered the Roman epistle written by Paul. It is believed to have been written while the apostle was at Corinth on his third missionary journey in A.D. 57 or 58. Cenchrea was the eastern harbor of Corinth, about nine miles from the city proper. Paul traveled via Cenchrea when he left Corinth (Acts 18:18) and could well have left the letter there for Phoebe to deliver.
  B. "Servant" comes from the Greek *diakonos* from which our word "deacon" comes. While Phoebe was a "deaconess" of the church in the sense that she served that congregation in some capacity, we know that she did not serve in the official office of a deacon because of the qualifications given in 1 Timothy 3:11 which restricts this office to males.

C. Dr. Lee Anna Star, in *The Bible Status of Women* conjectures that Phoebe was a minister as was Paul, Timothy, and others. This we know is a false assumption because:
  1. 1 Timothy 2:11-12 forbids it.
  2. Paul would have rebuked rather than commended her had she disobeyed the very thing he himself taught.

III. "Receive her in the Lord as becometh saints."
  A. Welcome her into their fellowship "in the Lord."
  B. Her reception was to be in a manner worthy of saints.

IV. "Assist her."
  A. The "business" with which she needed their assistance is not specified, and for us to guess what it was would serve no purpose.
  B. We can know it was a worthwhile matter because the apostle solicited their aid.
  C. Helping fellow Christians in whatever their needs should be the desire of every Christian.
  D. She had helped many, but now was in need of assistance herself. Roman saints were thus instructed to follow her example and help her in whatever manner was necessary and right in the executing of her mission.
    1. Rome was the capital of the world empire and Christians were not always treated kindly. If Phoebe needed protection, the saints were to provide it just as she had done for others.

V. "A succorer of many and myself also."
  A. "Succorer" is a feminine form of *prostates* which denotes a protectress, patroness; it is used metaphorically of Phoebe in Romans 16:2. It is a word of dignity, evidently chosen instead of others which might have been used (e.g., helper), and indicates the high esteem with which she was regarded, and one who had been a protectress of many" (W.E. Vine).
  B. This word suggests that Phoebe aided those who needed her and protected those who were oppressed. "Many" and "myself also" indicates the extent to which her services were rendered.

Dorcas (Acts 9:36-43)

I. Dorcas is the Greek form of the Aramaic name "Tabitha."

II. She lived in Joppa, the principle seacoast town of southern Palestine. Peter was here when he was called to go to Cornelius.

III. Peter's reputation in Joppa as a "miracle worker" was well founded.
   A. In the nearby city of Lydda he had healed Aeneas who had been suffering from palsy for eight years. This was a paralytic disease which was incurable by medical means.
   B. Naturally this event would enjoy widespread fame. It was a natural reaction for the friends of Dorcas to look to this source in their grief.

IV. Like Cornelius, Dorcas had the reputation of "giving much alms to the people" (Acts 9:36; 10:2).
   A. Dorcas was a living example of "Christianity at work."
   B. By her example we learn that there is something for all to do, regardless of how small we may consider our contribution.
   C. Jesus said, "The poor you always have with you" (John 12:8) indicating that opportunities to help them will always be available.
   D. James said, "Pure religion is to visit the fatherless and widows in their affliction" (Jas. 1:27). This is how Dorcas practiced "pure religion."
   E. Paul commanded that one "work with his hands the thing which is good that he may have to give to him that needeth" (Eph. 4:28).

VI. Dorcas' tools.
   A. A needle and threat—very small things but they accomplished great things.
   B. Like the widow who gave two mites into the treasury, which was all she had. Dorcas lives in history because she used wisely that which she had.

VII. Application.
   A. If we follow the example of Dorcas, we too will be "raise(d) from the   dead" from which there is no second death.
   B. Whether we sew for the poor, cook for the bereaved, or whatever we are able to do, it will be considered a great thing by God, if we

are motivated to do it with love in our hearts for God and our fellowman.

Questions

1. Lydia was of the city of _____.
2. Who wore purple in those days? _____
3. What were Lydia and her companions doing when encountered by the evangelists? _____
4. _____opened Lydia's heart. _____ opened her home.
5. By what means does God open one's heart? _____
   Does it require the cooperation of the one whose heart he opens (Rom. 10:9-10)? _____
6. Lydia and her companions were the first converts on the continent of _____ and in the city of_____.
7. How did Lydia show her faith (see Jas. 2:18) after she was baptized? _____

8. Phoebe was a servant of the _____ at _____.
9. She was commended to the saints at _____ by _____.
10. T____ F____ Phoebe served in the official office of a deacon. Prove your answer. _____
11. How was the church instructed to receive Phoebe?_____
    _____

12. Phoebe was a "succorer of _____ and of_____ also." Does this word suggest protection? _____
13. T____ F____ Dorcas and Tabitha were sisters in the flesh.
14. Friends of Dorcas called for _____ who was in Lydda at the time.
15. For what primary purpose were miracles performed (see Mark 16:20)?
    _____

    How does the Scripture say the raising of Dorcas accomplished this purpose (see Acts 10:42)?_____
    _____

16. T____ F____ Dorcas' example teaches us that all Christian women

Lydia, Phoebe, and Dorcas   57

must learn to sew "coats and garments" (v. 39) for widows. If your answer is "false," what does it teach? _____

17. We have entitled this lesson "Servants of God." In what ways did Lydia serve God? _____

    Phoebe? _____

    Dorcas?_____

18. List some things that we can learn from the example of these three women. _____
    _____
    _____
    _____

Lesson 12

Lois, Eunice, and Priscilla
"Teachers of Good Things"

Lois and Eunice (Acts 16:1; 2 Tim. 1:5)

I. Lois was the grandmother of Timothy, the evangelist; Eunice was Timothy's mother.
   A. Little is actually said of these women; they are mentioned by name only in 2 Timothy 1:5.
   B. They were Jews (Acts 16:1).
   C. Much is said of them through their son and grandson.

II. They possessed "unfeigned" (genuine) faith.
   A. They could not have taught Timothy that which they did not practice.
   B. One must first *do*, then teach (Acts 1:1).
   C. Whether both taught Timothy directly, or Lois taught Eunice who, in turn, taught him we do not know, but that both taught we cannot deny (2 Tim. 3:15).

III. The role of mothers in teaching their children.
   A. "Train up a child . . ." (Prov. 22:6).
   B. Widows indeed must have "brought up children" (1 Tim. 5:9-10).
   C. Example of parents taking their child to God (Luke 2:27).
   D. Teach them to obey parents "in the Lord" (Eph. 6:6).
   E. Example of evil instructions of a mother (Matt. 14:8).
   F. Good attributes of a mother (Prov. 31:10-31).
   G. Children are an "heritage of God." We must mold them in the right way (Ps.127:3).

IV. Timothy, the evangelist.
   A. Many things are said about this young man.
      1. Disciple of Christ (Acts 16:1).
      2. Fellowworker with Paul (Rom. 16:21).

3. Preacher of the gospel (2 Cor. 1:19; 1 Thess. 3:2).
   4. Trusted by the apostle Paul (Phil. 2:19-20).
   5. Did the work of the Lord (1 Cor. 16:19).
   6. Apparently imprisoned for the Lord's work (Heb. 13:23).
 B. Timothy's faith *first* dwelt in his grandmother and his mother. They live in history through his work.
   1. The worth of the teaching given to Timothy cannot be measured by any standard other than God's. The value of one soul is far above all the earth's treasures. No doubt countless thousands were influenced by the preaching of this outstanding evangelist.
   2. The teaching of God's way to *one* child can and often does result in the salvation of a multitude of souls. In nothing could our time be better spent than in teaching our children.

Priscilla

Acts 18:1-26; Romans 16:3; 2 Timothy 4:13; 1 Corinthians 16:19

I. Her home and occupation. Her original home was in Rome (Acts 18:2).
 A. She and her husband, Aquila, had been required to leave Rome because of a decree issued by Claudius, the Emperor of Rome, which expelled all Jews from that city. Claudius reigned from A.D. 41 to 53/54. The apostle Paul came to Corinth about A.D. 53.
 B. They were living in Corinth when Paul arrived there. Corinth was a well known city in Achaia (Greece).
 C. They were tentmakers. Paul, a fellow tentmaker, was invited by them to stay in their home (Acts 13:3).
 D. They left Corinth and went as far as Ephesus with Paul and his company (Acts 18:18-23). Paul left them there while he proposed to go to Jerusalem (Acts 18:19-21).

II. The teaching of Apollos.
 A. It was in Ephesus that they heard Apollos for the first time.
   1. He was an "eloquent man, mighty in the Scriptures" (OT).
   2. He knew only the baptism of John who taught that the kingdom was "at hand."
   3. Apollos was not aware that the kingdom had been established, thus he was practicing John's baptism which was in preparation for, and not in order to enter, the kingdom.

B. Priscilla and Aquila "took him unto them" and "expounded the way of the Lord more perfectly" (completely).
   1. We can only touch "the tip of the iceberg" in our knowledge of the extent to which this teaching reached.
   2. As it was with Timothy, so it was with Apollos. He became a mighty preacher of the gospel (see Acts 18:27-28; 1 Cor. 3:4-6; 4:6) and a fellow worker with Paul (1 Cor. 16:12; Tit. 3:13).
   3. How many were led to Christ by this eloquent man only God knows. This we do know: he was taught "the way of the Lord more perfectly" by these humble tentmakers.

III. Priscilla and Aquila returned to Rome.
   A. Claudius Caesar died in A.D. 53 or 54 at which time the edict against the Jews was apparently repealed. This enabled them to return to their native country.
      1. It is generally accepted by Bible scholars that the 1 Corinthian letter was written from Ephesus during Paul's two-year stay there (Acts 19:10) while on his third missionary journey (about A.D. 56).
      2. Either Aquila and Priscilla were with Paul in Ephesus when this letter was written or he had been in contact with them recently. This letter was written about a year before the Roman letter. It is most likely that they were still in Ephesus and returned to Rome sometime during the next year.
      3. At any rate, the greeting to the church at Corinth found in 1 Corinthians 16:19 is from them and the church in their house; not to them.
   B. They had returned to Rome by the time the Roman epistle was written (Rom. 16:3). This letter was written around A.D. 57 or 58.

IV. Priscilla's work and accomplishments serve as splendid examples for us.
   A. A valuable and industrious "help meet" for her husband.
   B. A teacher of "good things" (Tit. 2:3).
   C. A hospitable person (Acts 18:3; 1 Cor: 16:19).
      1. Paul was a recipient of this hospitality.
      2. The church met in her home in Rome and possibly in Ephesus also (Rom. 16:3; 1 Cor. 16:19).
   D. A faithful Christian (Rom. 16:3).

Lois, Eunice, and Priscilla

Questions

1. Lois was the _____ of Timothy; Eunice was his _____
2. Of what nationality were they? _____
3. T____ F____ Eunice began to teach Timothy when he reached "the age of accountability."
4. T____ F____ Timothy was circumcised "the eighth day" as was the custom of the Jews (see Acts 16:1-3). Explain your answer. _____
   _____
5. Define the kind of faith possessed by Lois, Eunice, and Timothy (see 2 Tim. 1:5). _____
6. Which Scriptures had Timothy known "from a child" (2 Tim. 3:15). _____ How do you know? _____
7. _____ called Timothy "my own son in the faith" (1 Tim. 1:2). Explain how this could be. _____
   _____
8. Children are an _____ of God (Ps. 127:3). What does this mean? _____
9. Because Aquila and Priscilla were _____, they were expelled from Rome by an imperial edict.
10. By occupation they were _____ as was the apostle Paul.
11. They encountered Apollos in _____
12. T____ F____ They taught Apollos that John's baptism was no longer valid.
13. If your answer to number 12 is "true," by what avenue did you arrive at that conclusion? _____
14. Apollos _____ (especially in Corinth) where Paul planted.
15. Paul left Aquila and Priscilla at _____ while he proposed to go to Jerusalem (see Acts 18:21).
16. Paul made _____ missionary journeys in addition to his preaching enroute to Rome as a prisoner. Here are the texts which mention the beginning of each journey:
    First journey (Acts 13:4).
    Second journey (Acts 15:41).

Third journey (Acts 18:23)
Upon which of these journeys did he meet Aquila and Priscilla for the first time? _____

17. Name two specific ways in which Priscilla demonstrated her hospitality. _____
18. Priscilla taught a *man* the way of the Lord more perfectly. Did she violate 1 Timothy 2:11-12? _____
    Explain your answer. _____
19. Name some characteristics and/or examples of Lois, Eunice, and Priscilla that we can apply to ourselves. _____
_____
_____
_____

Lesson 13

Wives of Rulers
Herodias, Pilate's Wife, Drusilla, Bernice

Herodias (Mark 6; Matt. 14; Luke 3)

According to history, Herodias was the grandaughter of Herod the Great who, among other heinous deeds, sought to destroy the child Jesus. The daughter of Aristobulus, she was first married to her half-uncle, Herod Philip and later to his half brother, Herod Antipas. It is to this Herod, the tetrarch of Galilee and Perea, that Jesus gave the name "Fox." This Herod was severely rebuked by John the Baptist for his adulterous union with Herodias.

Pilate sent Jesus to Herod Antipas prior to his crucifixion, hoping to ease tensions between himself and Herod (Luke 23:7-12).

Herodias' daughter by Herod Philip (Salome, according to Josephus) was a sensuous dancer who danced for Herod Antipas at his birthday celebration. She won his praise to the extent that he promised her anything she desired (Mark 6:22; Matt. 14:7). Salome was instructed by her mother to ask for the head of John the Baptist (Mark 6:24).

This is a classic example of the devastating results of an evil and vindictive heart. Destroying the life of the one who pronounces judgment does not change the judgment. It was just as "unlawful for thee (Herod) to have thy brother Philip's wife" (Matt. 14:4) after John was beheaded as it was before he was killed. Killing the preacher didn't make the truth go away.

Although Herod and Salome were accomplices in this horrible crime, they were merely tools in the hands of Herodias. As Jezebel used Ahab, so Herodias used her husband and daughter to accomplish her evil deed.

Herodias' story ends—so far as the Bible is concerned—with the beheading of John. However, history records her eventual banishment to Spain after the emperor Caligula took Antipas' official title of tetrarch from him (about A.D. 39). It is believed by historians that both Herod Antipas and Herodias died in exile in Spain.

Pilate's Wife (Matt. 27:19)

Pilate's wife was contemporary with Herodias. Tradition has named her Claudia Porcula, but the Bible refers to her only as Pilate's wife. We have no information regarding her personal background.

Although there are only thirty-eight words in the Bible about this woman (Matt. 27:19), she is known by Bible students the world over as one who recognized and appreciated the innocence of Jesus. Her story is told every time we study about Jesus' trial and subsequent crucifixion.

In contrast to Herodias, who sentenced the just John to death, Pilate's wife pleaded for the release of the innocent Jesus. "Have thou nothing to do with that just man: for I have suffered many things this day in a dream because of him" was her courageous plea to her husband while he sat on the judgment seat. Pilate "took water, and washed his hands before the multitude, saying, I am innocent of the blood of this just person: see ye to it" (Matt. 27:24). But he was not innocent. He released Barabbas, a murderer, to the mob, had Jesus scourged, and then delivered him to be crucified (Matt. 27:26). His wife's advice may have caused him to think about what he was doing, but he did not follow through with actions. Thus he lives in history as the one who sentenced the innocent Son of God to the shameful death on the cross, while she is remembered for her compassionate plea to have him released.

Drusilla and Bernice
(Acts 24:24, 25; 25:13, 23; 26:39)

Drusilla and Bernice were sisters—daughters of Herod Agrippa I. The elder sister, Bernice, was married (or at least lived with) her brother, Herod Agrippa II. Drusilla was the wife of Felix, governor (or procurator) of Judea. Both women were Jews.

Drusilla had defied Jewish law in marrying Felix who was a Gentile. Josephus tells us that she had been lured to Felix from her first husband, King Aziz, but the Bible is silent about this. No doubt she, like Felix, was in need of a sermon on "righteous, temperance and judgment to come" which the apostle Paul so ably delivered. Unlike Felix, her reaction is not stated in the Scriptures (Acts 24:25). So far as the record is concerned, neither she nor Felix ever had a "convenient season" to obey the Lord. Paul had no intentions of "bribing" Felix to release him, but rather used the "frequent" opportunities (when he was called before Felix) to preach the gospel of Christ. Eventually, to "gain favor with the Jews," Felix "left Paul in bonds" (see Acts 24:1-27).

Wives of Rulers

Bernice is introduced to us in Acts 25:13 when she came with her husband to Caesarea "to salute Festus." Festus had replaced Felix as governor (Acts 24:27). Like her sister before her, Bernice heard the great apostle plead his case. Paul had been wrongfully accused by the Jews of, among other things, having taken a Gentile into the temple (Acts 22:28-29). This Jewish mob proceeded to take him with the intent of killing him. He was rescued from the mob by Claudius Lysias who eventually sent him to Felix. He was permitted to make his defense before (1) the Sanhedrin Council (Acts 23:1-9); (2) Felix (Acts 24:10-25); (3) Festus (Acts 25:6-11); (4) King Agrippa II (Acts 26:1-27); and finally to Caesar himself (Acts 25:11-12).

Bernice heard Paul speak of the resurrection. She heard him say he had been sent by Christ to turn the people "from darkness to light" and "from the power of Satan unto God" (Acts 26:18). Agrippa was "almost persuaded to be a Christian"—so convincing were Paul's words (Acts 26:28), but of Bernice no such declaration was made. Although she was apparently convinced that "this man doeth nothing worthy of death or of bonds" (Acts 26:31), she did nothing to try to change either Paul's situation or her own incestuous life. She simply disappeared in obscure history as one of the most shameless women of her time.

Questions

1. Herodias was the daughter of _____, the son of Herod the Great.

2. She was married first to Herod _____ and later to his half-brother, Herod_____.

3. Define "tetrarch." _____

4. Why did John rebuke Herod and of what were he and Herodias guilty? _____

5. Salome's father and mother were _____ and _____.

6. What was the occasion when Salome danced for Herod? _____

7. T____ F____ When Herod heard Salome's request he regretted his promise to give her whatever she desired (Matt. 14:7-9; Mark 6:25).

8. For what is Pilate's wife famous?_____

   _____

9. T____ F____ The story of Jesus' trial and subsequent death is incomplete if Pilate's wife is excluded.

10. T____ F____ Pilate's wife was evidently concerned about her husband's dealing fairly with prisoners

11. Drusilla was the daughter of _____ and the sister of _____ and _____.

12. Drusilla was married to _____, procurator of Judea.

13. Define "procurator." _____

14. Bernice's husband was also her _____. What was his name?

    _____

15. T____ F____ Both Drusilla and Bernice heard John the Baptist plead his case.

16. Herod _____ had John the Baptist beheaded and Herod _____ heard Paul make his defense.

www.ingramcontent.com/pod-product-compliance
Lightning Source LLC
Chambersburg PA
CBHW061343040426
42444CB00011B/3062